Cursive Handwriting Workbook for Adults

The way to get started is to quit talking and start doing.

You are never too old to set another goal or dream another...

1 -2 -3
1. Learn Letters
2. Blend Words
3. Write Sentences

Comprehensive Learning and Practice Workbook
with Inspiring and Motivating Quotes

Introduction to Cursive Writing

Learning and practicing cursive writing is a worthwhile goal. Even with today's reliance on technology, sending or receiving a handwritten letter, note, or card is special. In addition, studies show that writing things out by hand aids in learning and recall. As an adult, it has probably been many years since you were taught cursiving handwriting. Likewise, our increasing dependence on computers and keyboards has left many people with poor cursive writing skills and illegible handwriting. This workbook is intended to help you improve your cursive writing skills in an easy and rewarding manner.

This *Cursive Handwriting Workbook for Adults* is designed to refresh and perfect your cursive penmanship skills in a way that is suited to adult learners. First, each letter of the alphabet is reviewed with emphasis on proper stroke technique. Next, practice blending letters together into words. Finally, perfect your cursive handwriting skills by tracing and then copying full sentences of inspirational and motivational quotations.

Before getting started, keep these general cursive writing tips in mind:

Hold your pen or pencil correctly. You should hold your pen so it is resting on your middle finger with your index finger and thumb holding it in place. Do not squeeze too tightly. Keep your grip loose to avoid straining the muscles in your hand.

Paper placement. Place your paper in front of you with the bottom left and top right corners aimed at the center of your chest (for right-handed people) or with the bottom right and top left corners aimed at the center of your chest (for left-handed people). Use your non-writing hand to hold the paper. Placing the paper on the diagonal like this will help facilitate the proper slant of your letters.

Don't press down too hard. There is no need to apply too much pressure when writing. This will only lead to hand strain and ugly-looking handwriting. Keep your hand light and loose.

Take your time. Writing too fast will cause your handwriting to become sloppy. Don't rush, instead focus on making each letter and word neatly and correctly. With time and practice, your handwriting will naturally speed up as your muscle memory increases.

Practice every day. Focus and consistency are key to perfecting your penmanship. Set aside time every day, 10-15 minutes, to work on the exercises in this book.

Uppercase Cursive Alphabet

Lowercase Cursive Alphabet

a b c d e f g h
i j k l m n o p
q r s t u v w x
y z 1 2 3 4 5 6 7 8 9 0

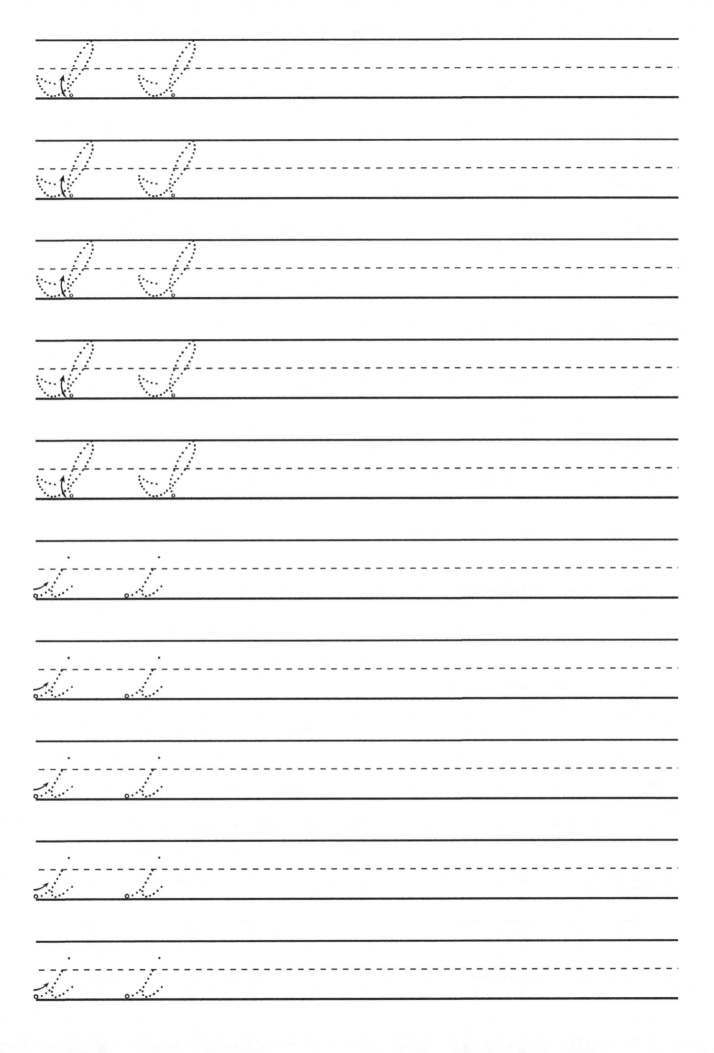

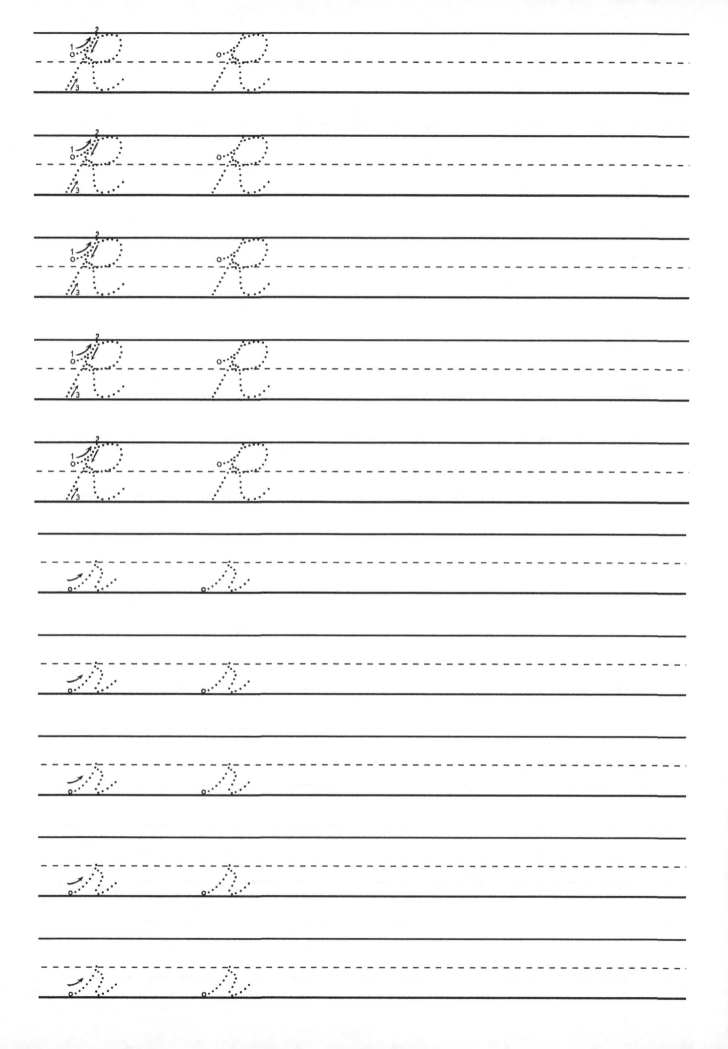

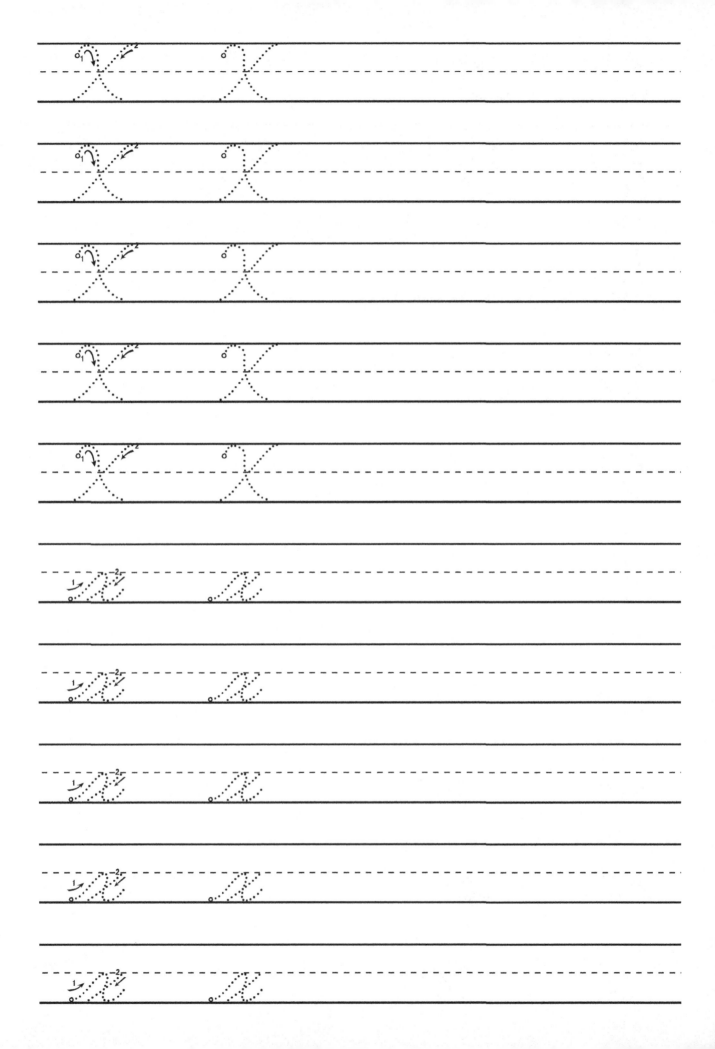

Part II

Words and Sentences

Practice blending letters together by first writing words
and then sentences.

Seem Seem

fool fool

try try

leave leave

Call Call

in in

from from

about about

time time

Person Person

year year

Way Way

Day Day

thing thing

man man

World World

life life

hand hand

Part Part

child child

eye eye

woman woman

Place Place

week week

and and

case case

They They

point point

That That

number number

good good

First First

Could Could

last last

great great

little little

The The

because because

would would

When When

and and

Your Your

different different

small small

public public

Same Same

make make

Be Be

apple apple

Adult Adult

burden burden

Write Write

process process

Draft Draft

find find

College College

wonder wonder

Easy Easy

quick quick

Transfer Transfer

July July

read read

ideas ideas

effective effective

exam exam

Critical Critical

outcome outcome

authentic authentic

Source Source

specific specific

Include Include

mother mother

handbook handbook

Others Others

uses uses

December December

Halloween Halloween

birthday birthday

clean clean

writing writing

through through

Time Time

meeting meeting

night night

activity activity

baseball baseball

fields fields

Whatever Whatever

together together

clubs clubs

Internet Internet

library library

teacher teacher

School School

consider consider

follow follow

beacon beacon

diversity diversity

Boston Boston

Tuesday Tuesday

monthly monthly

letters letters

integrate

proposal

business business

Friends Friends

information information

bias bias

take take

think think

look look

Want Want

use use

Find Find

tell tell

work work

over over

Into Into

after after

by by

Access Access

boss boss

chain chain

Decide Decide

Editor Editor

either either

fear fear

fewer fewer

garden garden

Gather Gather

heart heart

Hello Hello

imagine imagine

Impose Impose

Judge Judge

lady lady

market market

Math Math

nobody nobody

Nurse Nurse

Occupy Occupy

okay okay

payment payment

People People

quarter quarter

Quit Quit

raise raise

Really Really

Season Season

sauce sauce

testify testify

Thirty Thirty

Upon Upon

united united

veteran veteran

Virus Virus

West West

whisper whisper

youth youth

gone gone

Zoo Zoo

Seven Seven

The future belongs to those who

believe in the beauty of their dreams.

Tough times never last, but tough

people do.

Being confident means believing

in yourself.

The best way to predict the future

is to create it.

Nothing is particularly hard if you
break it down into small jobs.

The way to get started is to quit
talking and begin doing.

You learn more from failure than
from success.

It's not whether you get knocked
down, it's whether you get up.

Whether you think you can or you think you can't, you're right.

The only limits to our realization of tomorrow will be our doubts of today.

You are never too old to set another

goal or to dream a new dream.

To see what is right and not to do it

is a lack of courage.

Act as if you have all the confidence
you require until it becomes reality.

For every reason it's not possible,
there are hundreds of people who have
faced the same circumstances and
succeeded.

Those who are crazy enough to think

they can change the world do.

If I cannot do great things then I

can do small things in a great way.

Don't let yesterday take up too
much of today.

Wishing is not enough, we must do.

Do what you can with all you have,

wherever you are.

Reading is to the mind as exercise

is to the body.

Today's accomplishments were
yesterday's impossibilities.

You don't have to be great to start
but you have to start to be great.

The struggle you're in today is
developing the strength you'll need
for tomorrow.

Some days you just have to create
your own sunshine.

Be gentle with yourself, you're doing

the best you can.

Appreciate the good people in your

life, they're hard to come by.

Don't change who you are for

anyone.

You are powerful, beautiful, brilliant,

and brave.

The darkest nights produce the
the brightest stars.

Never hope for it more than you
work for it.

A few nice words can help a person

a lot more than you think.

Your value doesn't decrease based on

another's inability to see your worth.

Hard times will always reveal
true friends.

Difficult roads often lead to
beautiful destinations.

Nothing holds you back more than
your own insecurities.

Talk about your blessings more than
you talk about your burdens.

Mistakes are proof that you are trying.

You must do the thing you think you cannot do.

Surround yourself with people who
are only going to lift you higher.

The only person who is going to give
you the life you want is you.

Every saint has a past, every sinner

has a future.

When life knocks you down, roll

over and look at the stars.

The time is always right to do what
is right.

You know you have made the right
decision when there is peace in your
heart.

Don't rush and never settle. If it's
meant to be it will be.

Sometimes you're not given what
you want because something better
is planned for you instead.

I will not stress myself about things

I cannot control or change.

Expect nothing and appreciate

everything.

You never know how strong you
are until being strong is the only
choice you have.

If we wait until we are ready, we'll
be waiting the rest of our lives.

Never regret something that made

you smile.

Fill you're mind with positive

thoughts and watch your life change.

Life only comes around once, so do what makes you happy.

Train yourself to find the blessing in everything.

I'm going to make the rest of my
life the best of my life.

One small positive thought in the
morning can change your whole day.

If you stumble make it part of the dance.

Accept what is, let go of what was, have faith in what will be.

You don't need to have it all figured
out to move forward.

Every day may not be good, but
there is something good in every day.

Be strong, you never know who you
are inspiring.

Amazing things happen when you
distance yourself from negativity.

Stop holding yourself back. If you're
not happy, make a change.

Forgive them even if they're not
sorry.

Once you choose hope, anything is possible.

I'm not telling you it's going to be easy, I'm telling you it's going to be worth it.

What feels like the end is often the
beginning.

You may have to fight a battle more
than once to win it.

Strong people don't put others down,
they lift them up.

Life has a way of working out just
when you think it never will.

It's okay to not be okay all the

time.

Stop being afraid of what could go

wrong and think about what could

go right.

Made in the USA
Columbia, SC
28 September 2023